The Ultimate Muffin Guide

Brad .U Nielsen

Introduction

Embark on a delectable journey with this book, a treasure trove of diverse and mouthwatering muffin recipes that cater to every palate and craving. This massive collection showcases an array of flavors, textures, and creative combinations that elevate the humble muffin into a delightful culinary experience. Without explicitly mentioning the titles of each section, let's explore the vast world of muffins that awaits within the pages of this cookbook.

Dive into the rich and indulgent realm with choices like Chocoholic Muffins, Doughnut Muffins, and Chocolate Cheesecake Muffins. Embrace wholesome goodness with Whole Wheat Apple Muffins, Bran Muffins, and Healthy Blueberry and Banana Muffins. Experience the perfect balance of sweet and savory with options like Banana Crumb Muffins, Raspberry Corn Muffins, and Meatloaf Muffins.

For those who enjoy a touch of uniqueness, explore unconventional selections such as Jam Surprise Muffins, Matcha Muffins, and Baklava Muffins. Indulge in the comforting flavors of classics like Pumpkin Muffins, Blueberry Buttermilk Muffins, and Lemon Yogurt Muffins.

The cookbook also offers inventive combinations like Pizza Muffins, Monkey Bread Muffins, and Scrambled Egg Muffins, showcasing the versatility of this beloved baked treat.

Whether you're a seasoned baker or a novice in the kitchen, this book invites you to explore the art of muffin-making with creativity and flair. From sweet to savory, traditional to unconventional, this collection ensures that there's a muffin for every mood and occasion. Happy baking!

Contents

1. Chocoholic Muffins

***Serves 1*2**

What you'll need:

1 stick (1/2 cup) unsalted butter, melted and cooled
2 large eggs
1 cup low fat buttermilk
2 teaspoons vanilla extract
1-3/4 cups all-purpose flour, spooned into a measuring cup
2/3 cup unsweetened cocoa powder (not Dutch processed)
1-1/4 cups light brown sugar, packed (no hard lumps)
1 teaspoon baking powder
1 teaspoon baking soda
1/2 teaspoon salt
3/4 - 1 cup semi-sweet or bittersweet chocolate chips, to taste

What to do:

Position a rack in the center of the oven and preheat to 425 F. Spray a standard 12-cup muffin pan with nonstick cooking spray, and line with paper liners.

In a large measuring cup or bowl, whisk together the eggs, buttermilk, and vanilla extract.

In another large bowl, whisk together the flour, cocoa powder, brown sugar, baking powder, baking soda, and salt. Stir in the chocolate chips.

Add the wet ingredients and the melted butter to the dry ingredients and fold together with a rubber spatula until just combined. Don't over-mix the batter or the muffins will be tough (it's okay to leave a few specks of dry mixture).

Using an ice cream scoop or two spoons, fill the muffin cups to the brim with batter. Place in the oven and bake for 8 minutes, then turn the oven down to 350 F and bake for about 12 minutes more, or until a toothpick inserted in the center of a muffin comes out clean (check a few spots as the melted chocolate chips will make the tester look wet). Transfer to a wire rack and let cool for about 5 minutes before removing the muffins from the pan; cool on a rack.

2. Doughnut Muffins

Serves 12

What you'll need:

For Muffin Batter:

1 cup milk (low-fat works)
2 teaspoons lemon juice
12 tablespoons (1-1/2 sticks) unsalted butter, softened
1 cup granulated sugar
2 large eggs
1-1/2 teaspoons vanilla extract
3 cups all-purpose flour, spooned into measuring cup
2-1/2 teaspoons baking powder
1/4 teaspoon baking soda
1 teaspoon salt
2 teaspoons grated nutmeg

For Muffin Topping:

3 tablespoons unsalted butter
3 tablespoons granulated sugar
2-1/4 teaspoons cinnamon

What to do:

In a stand mixer or large bowl, beat the butter and sugar until light and fluffy, about 2 minutes. Beat in the eggs, one at a time, until just mixed in. Stir in the vanilla.

In a medium bowl, combine the flour, baking powder, baking soda, salt, and nutmeg. Stir with a whisk until well combined.

Using a rubber spatula, mix a quarter of the dry ingredients into the butter mixture. Then mix in a third of the milk mixture. Continue mixing in the remaining dry and wet ingredients alternately, ending with the dry. Mix until well combined and smooth, but don't over-mix. The batter will be very thick.

Scoop enough batter into each tin so that the top of the batter is even with the rim of the cup. Bake the muffins until firm to the touch, 25-30 minutes. Set pan on rack to cool for a few minutes.

Prepare the topping: melt the butter in a small dish and combine the cinnamon and sugar in another small dish.

When the muffins are cool enough to handle, use a pastry brush to paint the top of each muffin with butter, then sprinkle generously with cinnamon-sugar. If you have cinnamon-sugar left over, sprinkle muffins again. Serve warm, or cool on a rack.

3. Whole Wheat Apple Muffins

Serves 18

What you'll need:

1 cup (4 ounces) whole wheat flour
1 cup (4 1/4 ounces) all-purpose flour
1 teaspoon baking powder
1 teaspoon baking soda
1/4 teaspoon salt
1 tablespoon cinnamon
1/2 cup (4 ounces) unsalted butter, at room temperature
1/2 cup (3 1/2 ounces) granulated sugar
1/2 cup dark brown sugar, packed, divided
1 large egg, lightly beaten
1 cup (8 ounces) buttermilk or yogurt
2 large apples, peeled, cored, and coarsely chopped

What to do:

Preheat the oven to 450 F. Grease and flour 18 muffin cups and set aside.

Mix together the flours, baking powder, baking soda, salt, and cinnamon, and set aside. In a separate bowl, cream the butter and add the granulated sugar and 1/4 cup of the brown sugar. Beat until fluffy.

Add the egg and mix well; stop once to scrape the sides and bottom of the bowl. Mix in the buttermilk gently. (Don't over-mix, the buttermilk will cause the mixture to curdle.) Stir in the dry ingredients and fold in the apple chunks.

Divide the batter evenly among the prepared muffin cups, sprinkling the remaining 1/4 cup brown sugar on top. Bake for 10 minutes, turn the heat down to 400 F, and bake for an additional 5 to 10 minutes, or until a toothpick inserted into the center of a muffin comes out clean. Cool the muffins for 5 minutes in the tin, then turn them out onto a wire rack to cool completely.

4. Cornbread Muffins

Serves 12

What you'll need:

3/4 cup yellow cornmeal
1-1/4 cups all-purpose flour, spooned into a measuring cup
1 tablespoon baking powder
1/2 cup sugar
1 teaspoon salt
2 large eggs
2 tablespoons honey
3/4 cup milk (whole works best but low-fat is OK too)
1 stick (1/2 cup) unsalted butter, at room temperature

What to do:

Preheat the oven to 350 F. spray a muffin pan with non-stick cooking spray.

In a large bowl, whisk together the cornmeal, flour, baking powder, sugar and salt.

In a separate bowl, break up the eggs with a whisk. Whisk in the honey and then the milk. Add the milk mixture and melted butter to the dry ingredients. Stir until just blended. Do not over-mix; a few lumps are OK. Spoon the batter evenly into the prepared muffin pan, filling each cup almost full. Bake for 17-20 minutes, or until the tops are set and golden. Cool the muffins for a few minutes in the pan, then serve warm.

5. Perfect Blueberry Muffins

Serves 10

What you'll need:

5 tablespoons unsalted butter, softened
1/2 cup (3 1/2 ounces) sugar
1 large egg
3/4 cup sour cream or plain yogurt
1/2 teaspoon grated lemon zest
1 1/2 cups (6 3/4 ounces) all-purpose flour
1 1/2 teaspoon baking powder
1/4 teaspoon baking soda
1/4 teaspoon salt
3/4 cup blueberries, fresh or frozen (if frozen, you don't need to defrost)

What to do:

Preheat oven to 375 F. Line a muffin tin with 10 paper liners or spray each cup with a nonstick spray.

Beat butter and sugar with an electric mixer until light and fluffy. Add egg and beat well, then yogurt and zest. Put flour, baking powder, baking soda and salt into a sifter and sift half of dry ingredients over batter. Mix until combined. Sift remaining dry ingredients into batter and mix just until the flour disappears.

Gently fold in your blueberries. The dough will be quite thick. They should be about 3/4 full, nothing more, so you might only need 9 instead of 10 cups.

Bake for 25 to 30 minutes, until tops are golden and a tester inserted into the center of muffins comes out clean (except for blueberry goo). Let cool on rack.

6. Banana Crumb Muffins

Serves 10

What you'll need:

1 1/2 cups all-purpose flour
1 teaspoon baking soda
1 teaspoon baking powder
1/2 teaspoon salt
3 bananas, mashed
3/4 cup white sugar
1 egg, lightly beaten
1/3 cup butter, melted
1/3 cup packed brown sugar
2 tablespoons all-purpose flour
1/8 teaspoon ground cinnamon
1 tablespoon butter

What to do:

Preheat oven to 375 degrees F (190 degrees C). Lightly grease 10 muffin cups, or line with muffin papers.

In a large bowl, mix together 1 1/2 cups flour, baking soda, baking powder and salt. In another bowl, beat together bananas, sugar, egg and melted butter. Stir the banana mixture into the flour mixture just until moistened. Spoon batter into prepared muffin cups.

In a small bowl, mix together brown sugar, 2 tablespoons flour and cinnamon. Cut in 1 tablespoon butter until mixture resembles coarse cornmeal. Sprinkle topping over muffins.

Bake in preheated oven for 18 to 20 minutes, until a toothpick inserted into center of a muffin comes out clean.

7. Killer Blueberry Muffins

Serves 8

What you'll need:

1 1/2 cups all-purpose flour
3/4 cup white sugar
1/2 teaspoon salt
2 teaspoons baking powder
1/3 cup vegetable oil
1 egg
1/3 cup milk
1 cup fresh blueberries
1/2 cup white sugar
1/3 cup all-purpose flour
1/4 cup butter, cubed
1 1/2 teaspoons ground cinnamon

What to do:

Preheat oven to 400 degrees F (200 degrees C). Grease muffin cups or line with muffin liners.

Combine 1 1/2 cups flour, 3/4 cup sugar, salt and baking powder. Place vegetable oil into a 1 cup measuring cup; add the egg and enough milk to fill the cup. Mix this with flour mixture. Fold in blueberries. Fill muffin cups right to the top, and sprinkle with crumb topping mixture.

To Make Crumb Topping: Mix together 1/2 cup sugar, 1/3 cup flour, 1/4 cup butter, and 1 1/2 teaspoons cinnamon. Mix with fork, and sprinkle over muffins before baking.

Bake for 20 to 25 minutes in the preheated oven, or until done.

8. Seminary Muffins

Serves 12

What you'll need:

1 egg
1 1/3 cups mashed ripe banana
3/4 cup packed brown sugar
1/3 cup applesauce
1 teaspoon vanilla extract
1 cup all-purpose flour
1/2 teaspoon baking soda
2 teaspoons baking powder
1 1/4 teaspoons salt
1 teaspoon ground cinnamon
1 cup quick cooking oats
1/2 cup semisweet chocolate chips
1/2 cup chopped walnuts

What to do:

Preheat oven to 350 degrees F (175 degrees C). Lightly grease one 12 cup muffin pan.

In a large bowl, combine egg, banana, brown sugar, applesauce and vanilla. In a separate bowl, sift together flour, baking soda, baking powder, salt and cinnamon.

Gently stir flour mixture and oatmeal into banana mixture. Fold in chocolate chips and walnuts. Pour batter into prepared muffin cups.

Bake in preheated oven or 15 to 20 minutes, or until light brown. Remove muffins from pan and place on a wire rack to let cool before serving.

9. Rhubarb Muffins

Serves 12

What you'll need:

1/2 cup vanilla yogurt
2 tablespoons butter, melted
2 tablespoons vegetable oil
1 egg
1 1/3 cups all-purpose flour
3/4 cup brown sugar
1/2 teaspoon baking soda
1/4 teaspoon salt
1 cup diced rhubarb

1/4 cup brown sugar
1/2 teaspoon ground cinnamon
1/4 teaspoon ground nutmeg
1/4 cup crushed sliced almonds
2 teaspoons melted butter

What to do:

Preheat the oven to 350 degrees F (175 degrees C). Grease a 12 cup muffin tin, or line with paper liners.

In a medium bowl, stir together the yogurt, 2 tablespoons of melted butter, oil and egg. In a large bowl, stir together the flour, 3/4 cup of brown sugar, baking soda and salt. Pour the wet ingredients into the dry, and mix until just blended. Fold in rhubarb. Spoon into the prepared muffin tin, filling cups at least 2/3 full.

In a small bowl, stir together 1/4 cup of brown sugar, cinnamon, nutmeg, almonds, and 2 teaspoons of melted butter. Spoon over the tops of the muffins, and press down lightly.

Bake for 25 minutes in the preheated oven, or until the tops spring back when lightly pressed. Cool in the pan for about 15 minutes before removing.

10. Millet Muffins

Serves 16

What you'll need:

2 1/4 cups whole wheat flour
1/3 cup millet
1 teaspoon baking powder
1 teaspoon baking soda
1 teaspoon salt
1 cup buttermilk
1 egg, lightly beaten
1/2 cup vegetable oil
1/2 cup honey

What to do:

Preheat oven to 400 degrees F (200 degrees C). Grease 16 muffin cups.

In a large bowl, mix the whole wheat flour, millet flour, baking powder, baking soda, and salt. In a separate bowl, mix the buttermilk, egg, vegetable oil, and honey. Stir buttermilk mixture into the flour mixture just until evenly moist. Transfer batter to the prepared muffin cups.

Bake 15 minutes in the preheated oven, or until a toothpick inserted in the center of a muffin comes out clean.

11. Sweet Muffins

Serves 12

What you'll need:

1 egg
1/2 cup milk
1/4 cup vegetable oil
1 1/2 cups all-purpose flour
1/2 cup white sugar
2 teaspoons baking powder
1/2 teaspoon salt

What to do:

Preheat oven to 400 degrees F (205 degrees C).

Grease muffin cups or use papers. Beat egg with a fork. Stir in milk and oil. Sift flour and measure. Add sugar, baking powder and salt. Add egg mixture to flour and stir until flour is moistened. BATTER SHOULD BE LUMPY. DO NOT OVERMIX.

Fill muffin cups 2/3 full. Bake 20 to 25 minutes until golden brown. Muffins should have rounded and pebbled tops. Serve warm.

12. Huckleberry Muffins

Serves 15

What you'll need:

3/4 cup butter
1 cup white sugar
1 egg
3/4 cup milk
1 teaspoon vanilla extract
1 3/4 cups sifted all-purpose flour
2 1/2 teaspoons baking powder
1/2 teaspoon salt
1 cup huckleberries
1 tablespoon all-purpose flour

What to do:

Preheat the oven to 400 degrees F (200 degrees C). Grease 15 muffin cups, or line with muffin papers.

In a large bowl, cream together the butter and sugar until smooth. Mix in the egg, milk and vanilla until well blended. Combine 1 3/4 cups flour, baking powder and salt; stir into the batter until just moistened. Toss huckleberries with remaining flour to coat, then fold them into the batter. Spoon batter into muffin cups, filling at least 2/3 full.

Bake for 15 minutes in the preheated oven, or until the tops spring back when lightly pressed.

13. Apricot Muffins

Serves 12

What you'll need:

1 cup chopped dried apricots
1 cup boiling water
2 cups all-purpose flour
3/4 cup white sugar
1 teaspoon baking soda
1/2 teaspoon salt
1/4 cup melted butter
1/4 cup vegetable oil
1 cup buttermilk
1 egg

What to do:

Preheat the oven to 400 degrees F (200 degrees C). Grease a 12 cup muffin pan, or line with paper muffin cups. Place apricots into a small bowl, and pour the boiling water over them. Let stand for 5 minutes.

In a medium bowl stir together the flour, sugar, baking soda and salt. In a separate bowl, whisk together the melted butter, oil, buttermilk and egg. Pour the wet ingredients into the dry ingredients, and stir until just blended. It is okay for the batter to have some lumps. Drain water from apricots, and mix them into the batter. Spoon into the prepared muffin cups.

Bake for 15 minutes in the preheated oven, or until the top springs back when lightly pressed. Cool in the pan over a wire rack.

14. Mormon Muffins

Serves 5 dozen

What you'll need:

2 cups boiling water
5 teaspoons baking soda
5 cups all-purpose flour
1 quart buttermilk
4 cups bran cereal (such as Kellogg's or All-Bran)
2 cups bran flakes cereal
1 cup chopped walnuts
1 cup white sugar
1/2 cup vegetable oil
1/2 cup butter, melted
4 eggs, beaten
2 teaspoons ground cinnamon
1 teaspoon salt
1/2 teaspoon ground ginger
1/2 teaspoon nutmeg

What to do:

Combine boiling water and baking soda together in a large bowl. Let cool slightly.

Stir flour, buttermilk, bran cereal, bran flakes, walnuts, sugar, oil, butter, eggs, cinnamon, salt, ginger, and nutmeg into water-baking soda mixture until just combined. Cover bowl with plastic wrap and refrigerate muffin batter for at least 8 hours or overnight.

Preheat oven to 375 degrees F (190 degrees C). Grease 60 muffin cups or line with paper muffin liners.

Pour batter into prepared muffin cups 1/2 full.

Bake muffins in the preheated oven until the tops spring back when lightly pressed, about 20 minutes.

15. Quinoa Muffins

Serves 6

What you'll need:

Cooking spray
1 cup cooked quinoa
3 large eggs, beaten
1/4 cup crumbled feta cheese
1/4 cup sliced mushrooms
1/4 cup chopped onion
1/2 teaspoon dried thyme
Salt and ground black pepper to taste

What to do:

Preheat oven to 400 degrees F (200 degrees C). Prepare 6 muffin cups with cooking spray.

Beat quinoa, eggs, feta cheese, mushrooms, onion, thyme, salt, and pepper together in a large bowl. Spoon into prepared muffin cups to about halfway full.

Bake in the preheated oven until edges brown and the tops are firm to the touch, 20 to 30 minutes.

16. Beer Muffins

Serves 10

What you'll need:

3 cups buttermilk baking mix
2 tablespoons white sugar
1 cup chopped raisins
1 cup beer

What to do:

Preheat oven to 350 degrees F (175 degrees C). Lightly grease 10 muffin cups.

In a large bowl, combine baking mix, sugar, raisins and beer; stir until smooth. Don't over-mix. Pour batter into greased muffin cups.

Bake in preheated oven until golden brown, about 15 minutes.

17. Teff Muffins

Serves 12

What you'll need:

3/4 cup teff flour
3/4 cup brown rice flour
1/2 cup arrowroot flour
1 1/2 teaspoons baking powder
1/2 teaspoon ground cinnamon
1/4 teaspoon ground nutmeg
1/4 teaspoon ground cloves
1/4 teaspoon ground ginger
1/4 teaspoon salt
2/3 cup water
1/2 cup chopped pecans
1/3 cup olive oil
2 eggs, beaten
1/2 cup raisins
1/2 cup golden raisins
1/2 cup dried apricots, chopped
1/2 cup dried cranberries

What to do:

Preheat oven to 400 degrees F (200 degrees C). Grease a muffin tin.

Mix teff flour, brown rice flour, arrowroot flour, baking powder, cinnamon, nutmeg, cloves, ginger, and salt together in a large bowl. Form a well in the center of the flour mixture. Add water, pecans, olive oil, and eggs to the well. Whisk the wet ingredients into the dry ingredients until batter is fully combined. Fold raisins, golden raisins, apricots, and cranberries into batter. Pour batter into the prepared muffin tin.

Bake in the preheated oven until a toothpick inserted into the center of a muffin comes out clean, about 25 minutes.

18. Jam Surprise Muffins

Serves 4

What you'll need:

1 1/3 cups whole wheat flour
1/3 cup wheat germ
1 teaspoon baking powder
1/2 teaspoon baking soda
1 teaspoon salt
1/2 cup brown sugar
1/3 cup butter, melted
1 egg
1 cup buttermilk
1/4 cup any flavor fruit jam

What to do:

Preheat oven to 425 degrees F (220 degrees C). Grease muffin cups or line with paper muffin liners.

Stir together flour, wheat germ, baking powder, salt and brown sugar. In a separate bowl, mix together butter, egg and buttermilk. Stir milk mixture into dry ingredients; mix just until combined. Fill prepared muffin cups half full with batter. Make a depression in the center of each muffin and drop in 1 teaspoon of jam. Cover jam with additional batter.

Bake in preheated oven for 20 to 25 minutes.

19. Matcha Muffins

Serves 6

What you'll need:

3/4 cup cake flour, about 4 ounces
1 tablespoon baking powder
1 tablespoon matcha
2 tablespoons powdered sugar
1/2 cup soy milk, freshly extracted or purchased
1 tablespoon maple syrup
Drop of soy sauce, preferably light-colored soy sauce
1/4 teaspoon vegetable oil (optional)
2 tablespoons drained Sweet Black Beans (optional)

What to do:

Sift together the cake flour, baking powder, matcha, and powdered sugar into a bowl. Set aside.

In a separate bowl, whisk the soy milk until foamy. Add the maple syrup and soy sauce and continue to whisk and incorporate air. Add the vegetable oil if your soy milk is not especially "rich."

Resift the flour mixture. Fold it into the soy milk mixture in two or three batches, stirring gently after each addition to combine. The resulting batter should be smooth, thick, and slightly foamy. Line individual freestanding cupcake forms, or a 6-muffin tin (if it will fit in your steamer), with paper or foil liners and pour in a scant 1/4 cup of the batter. Tap down to level the batter. If you are using the black beans, place 6 or 7 beans on top of the batter in each cup (the weight of the beans will cause them to sink).

Place the filled cups in a flat-bottomed, lidded steamer fitted with a cloth-protected lid. Set the steamer over high heat. Once you hear the water boiling, adjust the heat to maintain a steady flow of steam. Steam for 15 to 20 minutes, or until the tops of the muffins crack and split and a toothpick inserted into the center of a muffin comes out clean. Always remove the lid carefully to avoid the steam burning your hand.

Transfer the muffins to a rack to cool.

20. Oatmeal Muffins

Serves 1

What you'll need:

Nonstick vegetable oil spray
2 1/3 cups quick-cooking oats
1 cup whole wheat flour
1/2 cup chopped pecans (about 2 ounces)
1/2 cup (packed) dark brown sugar
1/2 cup sugar
2 tablespoons natural oat bran
2 tablespoons wheat germ
2 teaspoons ground cinnamon
1 1/2 teaspoons baking soda
3/4 teaspoon salt
1 cup buttermilk
1/2 cup canola oil
1 large egg
1 teaspoon vanilla extract
1/3 cup boiling water
1 1/2 cups fresh or frozen wild blueberries

What to do:

Preheat oven to 375°F. Spray 8 large muffin cups (1-cup capacity) or 18 standard muffin cups (1/3-cup capacity) with nonstick spray. Whisk oats and next 9 ingredients in large bowl. Add buttermilk, oil, egg, and vanilla; whisk to blend. Stir in 1/3 cup boiling water and let stand 5 minutes. Fold in blueberries. Divide batter among prepared muffin cups.

Bake muffins until tester inserted into center comes out clean, about 28 minutes for large muffins and 20 minutes for standard muffins. Cool 10 minutes. Turn muffins out onto rack; cool. Serve warm or at room temperature.

21. Pumpkin Muffins

Serves 12

What you'll need:

Softened unsalted butter, for the pan
3 2/3 cups pastry flour, sifted
1 tablespoon plus 1 teaspoon baking powder
1 teaspoon ground cinnamon
1/4 teaspoon ground ginger
1/4 teaspoon freshly grated nutmeg
1/4 teaspoon fine sea salt
8 tablespoons (1 stick) unsalted butter, chilled and cut into 1/2-inch cubes
1 1/3 cups superfine sugar
4 large eggs, at room temperature, beaten
One 15-ounce can solid-pack pumpkin
1 cup seedless golden or dark raisins
1/4 cup hulled unsalted sunflower seeds

What to do:

Position a rack in the center of the oven and preheat to 400°F. Brush the insides of 12 to 14 muffin cups with softened butter, then brush the top of the pan.

Sift the flour, baking powder, cinnamon, ginger, nutmeg, and salt together into a medium bowl. Beat the butter in the bowl of a heavy-duty stand mixer fitted with the paddle attachment on high speed until creamy, about I minute.

Gradually beat in the sugar and continue beating, scraping the sides of the bowl often with a silicone spatula, until the mixture is very light in color and texture, about 5 minutes. Gradually beat in the eggs. Reduce the mixture speed to low.

Beat in the pumpkin; the mixture may look curdled. In thirds, beat in the flour mixture, scraping down the sides of the bowl often, and mix until smooth. Add the raisins. Increase the speed to high and beat until the batter has a slight sheen, about 15 seconds, no longer.

Using a 2 1/2 inch-diameter ice-cream scoop, portion the batter, rounded side up, into the prepared cups. Sprinkle the tops with the sunflower seeds.

Bake for 10 minutes. Reduce the oven temperature to 375°F and continue baking until the tops of the muffins are golden brown and a wire cake tester inserted into the center of a muffin comes out clean, about 15 minutes more.

Cool in the pan for 10 minutes. Remove the muffins from the pan and cool completely.

22. Linzer Muffins

Serves 12

What you'll need:

1 cup whole almonds, toasted and cooled completely
3/4 cup sugar
1/2 teaspoon finely grated fresh lemon zest
1 1/2 cups all-purpose flour
2 teaspoons baking powder
1/2 teaspoon salt
1/4 teaspoon cinnamon
1 cup whole milk
3/4 stick (6 tablespoons) unsalted butter, melted and cooled
1 large egg
1/8 teaspoon almond extract
About 1/3 cup seedless raspberry jam
Confectioners' sugar for dusting
A muffin tin with 12 (1/2-cup) muffin cups

What to do:

Put oven rack in middle position and preheat oven to 400°F. Grease muffin cups.

Grind almonds with sugar and zest in a food processor until almonds are finely ground.

Whisk together flour, almond mixture, baking powder, salt, and cinnamon in a large bowl. Whisk together milk, butter, egg, and almond extract in a small bowl, then stir into dry ingredients until combined.

Put a scant 1/4 cup batter into each muffin cup. Top each with 1 rounded teaspoon jam. Divide remaining batter among cups. Bake until golden and muffins pull away from edges of cups, about 20 minutes. Cool in pan on a rack 5 to 10 minutes, then turn out onto rack. Dust with confectioners' sugar before serving.

23. Parmesan Muffins

Serves 12

What you'll need:

2 large eggs
3/4 cup milk
1/2 cup extra-virgin olive oil
2 ounces freshly grated parmesan (1 cup)
1 1/2 cups all-purpose flour
2 tablespoons sugar
2 teaspoons baking powder
1/4 teaspoon baking soda
1 teaspoon finely chopped garlic
1 teaspoon finely chopped fresh rosemary
3/4 teaspoon salt
1/2 teaspoon black pepper

What to do:

Put oven rack in middle position and preheat oven to 350°F.

Whisk together eggs, milk, and oil in a bowl. Whisk together 3/4 cup cheese and all of remaining ingredients in a large bowl, then add wet ingredients to dry ingredients. Whisk until combined.

Divide among 12 greased (1/2-cup) muffin cups. Sprinkle with remaining 1/4 cup cheese and bake until a tester comes out clean, about 20 minutes. Cool in pan on a rack 5 to 10 minutes.

24. Mincemeat Muffins

Serves 12

What you'll need:

2 cups all-purpose flour
2/3 cup sugar
1 tablespoon baking powder
1/4 teaspoon salt
2 large eggs
1/2 cup whole milk
6 tablespoons (3/4 stick) unsalted butter, melted, cooled
1 tablespoon grated orange peel
2/3 cup purchased mincemeat from jar

What to do:

Preheat oven to 400°F. Line twelve 1/3-cup muffin cups with paper liners. Mix first 4 ingredients in large bowl. Whisk eggs, milk, butter and orange peel to blend in medium bowl; whisk in mincemeat. Add to dry ingredients; stir until just blended. Divide batter among prepared cups.

Bake until muffins are light golden brown and tester inserted into center comes out clean, about 25 minutes. Transfer to racks and cool slightly. Serve warm or at room temperature.

25. Carrot Muffins

Serves 18

What you'll need:

2 cups all-purpose flour
2 teaspoons baking soda
2 teaspoons cinnamon
1/4 teaspoon salt
1 1/4 cups sugar
1/4 pound carrots
1/2 cup pecans
1/2 cup raisins
1/4 cup sweetened flaked coconut
3 large eggs
1 cup corn oil
2 teaspoons vanilla
1 Granny Smith apple

What to do:

Preheat oven to 350°F. and oil eighteen 1/2-cup muffin cups.

Into a large bowl sift together flour, baking soda, cinnamon, and salt and whisk in sugar. Coarsely shred enough carrots to measure 2 cups and chop pecans. Add shredded carrots and pecans to flour mixture with raisins and coconut and toss well.

In a bowl whisk together eggs, oil, and vanilla. Peel and core apple and coarsely shred. Stir shredded apple into egg mixture and add to flour mixture, stirring until batter is just combined well. Divide batter among muffin cups, filling them three fourths full, and bake in middle of oven until puffed and a tester comes out clean, 15 to 20 minutes.

Cool muffins in cups on racks 5 minutes before turning out onto racks to cool completely. Muffins keep in an airtight container at room temperature 5 days.

26. Bran Muffins

Serves 9

What you'll need:

Vegetable-oil cooking spray
1 cup All-Bran fiber cereal
1 cup raisin bran cereal
1/4 cup skim milk
1 1/4 cups fresh orange juice
1 1/4 cups all-purpose flour
1 tablespoon baking powder
1/4 teaspoon cinnamon, or to taste
1/4 teaspoon salt
1 large egg white, beaten lightly
1/2 cup honey

What to do:

Preheat oven to 400°F and lightly coat nine 1/4-cup muffin tins with cooking spray.

In a large bowl combine cereals, milk, and orange juice and let stand 5 minutes. In a small bowl whisk together flour, baking powder, cinnamon, and salt. Into cereal mixture stir egg white and honey until combined well. Add flour mixture and stir until just combined.

Divide batter among muffin tins and bake in middle of oven 20 minutes, or until golden and a tester comes out clean. Turn muffins out onto racks and cool.

27. Limpa Muffins (Swedish Rye Bread Muffins)

Serves 12

What you'll need:

1 1/2 cups all-purpose flour
1 cup rye flour
1 tablespoon baking powder
1 teaspoon salt
1 1/4 teaspoons aniseed
1 1/4 teaspoons caraway seeds
1 cup milk
1 large egg
1 teaspoon freshly grated orange zest
1/2 stick (1/4 cup) unsalted butter, melted
2 1/2 tablespoons unsulfured molasses

What to do:

Preheat oven to 425°F. and butter twelve 1/3-cup muffin tins.

In a bowl whisk together flours, baking powder, salt, aniseed, and caraway seeds. In a small bowl whisk together milk, egg zest, butter, and molasses. Add milk mixture to flour mixture, stirring until just combined (do not over mix).

Divide batter evenly among muffin tins and bake in middle of oven 15 to 20 minutes, or until a tester comes out clean.

28. Pecan Muffins

Serves 10

What you'll need:

1 3/4 cups sifted all-purpose flour
1/2 cup sugar
1 teaspoon baking powder
1/2 teaspoon baking soda
1/2 teaspoon salt
1/2 cup sour cream
1/2 cup peach preserves
1 egg
1 teaspoon vanilla extract
2/3 cup chopped pecans, toasted

What to do:

Position rack in center of oven and preheat to 400°F. Line 10 muffin cups with muffin papers.

Sift first 5 ingredients into large bowl. Whisk sour cream, preserves, egg and vanilla to blend in medium bowl. Add sour cream mixture and pecans to dry ingredients and stir just until combined; do not overmix.

Divide batter among muffin cups. Bake until tester inserted into center of muffins comes out clean, about 20 minutes. Cool 15 minutes before serving.

29. Chocolate Chip Muffins

Serves 12

What you'll need:

2 cups all-purpose flour
1/3 cup light-brown sugar, packed
1/3 cup sugar
2 teaspoons baking powder
1/2 teaspoon salt
2/3 cup milk
1/2 cup butter, melted and cooled
2 eggs, lightly beaten
1 teaspoon vanilla
1 (11 1/2 ounce) package milk chocolate chips
1/2 cup walnuts or 1/2 cup pecans, chopped

What to do:

Preheat oven to 400°F and grease twelve muffin cups.

In a large bowl, stir together flour, sugars, baking powder, and salt.

In another bowl, stir together milk, eggs, butter, and vanilla until blended.

Make a well in center of dry ingredients, add milk mixture and stir just to combine. Stir in chocolate chips and nuts. Spoon batter into prepared muffin cups.

Now bake for 15-20 minutes or until a cake tester inserted in center of one muffin comes out clean.

Remove muffin tin to wire rack. Cool for 5 minutes. Remove from tins to finish cooling.

Serve warm or completely cool.

30. Apple Pie Muffins

Serves 18

What you'll need:

For the Topping:

1/2 cup firmly packed brown sugar
1/3 cup all-purpose flour
1/4 cup unsalted butter, melted
1 teaspoon cinnamon

For the Muffins:

1 1/2 cups firmly packed brown sugar
2/3 cup vegetable oil
1 egg
1 1/2 teaspoons vanilla
2 1/2 cups all-purpose flour
1 teaspoon baking soda
1/4 teaspoon salt
1 cup buttermilk
2 cups diced peeled firm tart apples (such as Spy or Granny Smith)

What to do:

Note: cinnamon could be added to the batter (about 1 teaspoon).

Topping: In a small bowl toss together sugar, flour, butter and cinnamon until crumbly; set aside.

Muffins: In a large bowl whisk together brown sugar, oil, egg and vanilla until smooth. In a separate bowl, sift together flour, soda and salt. Stir oil mixture into flour mixture alternately with buttermilk. Fold in apples, mixing just until combined.

Spoon into greased muffin cups filling 3/4 full and sprinkle topping over evenly.

Bake at 350°F for 25-30 minutes or until golden brown and tops spring back.

31. Banana-Chocolate Chip Muffins

Serves 12

What you'll need:

3 medium very ripe bananas
1 egg
1/3 cup low-fat buttermilk or 1/3 cup milk
1/2 cup granulated sugar
1/2 cup brown sugar
1 1/2 cups flour
1 teaspoon baking soda
1 teaspoon salt
2 -3 tablespoons chocolate chips
2 tablespoons chopped walnuts (optional)

What to do:

Preheat oven to 350 F.

Lightly coat 12 muffin tin liners with cooking spray and place in muffin tin.

In large bowl, mash bananas with fork.

Whisk in egg, milk, granulated sugar, and brown sugar.

In separate bowl, combine flour, baking soda, and salt.

Add flour mixture to banana mixture and combine well.

Fold in chocolate chips and walnuts.

Spoon equal amounts of batter into 12 muffin cups.

Bake 30 minutes or until toothpick inserted in center comes out clean.

Allow to cool slightly in pan, then remove to wire rack.

32. Strawberry Berry-Smash Muffins

Serves 12

What you'll need:

1 2/3 cups fresh strawberries
2/3 cup sugar
1/3 cup vegetable oil
2 eggs
1 1/2 cups Gold Medal all-purpose flour
1/2 teaspoon baking soda
1/2 teaspoon salt
1/2 teaspoon cinnamon

What to do:

Heat oven to 425 F.

Put a paper baking cup in each of 12 regular-size muffin cups, or grease just the bottoms of 12 muffin cups.

Slightly smash strawberries in large bowl, using fork.

Stir in sugar, oil and eggs until mixed.

Stir in other ingredients just until moistened.

Spoon batter into muffin cups.

Bake 15 to 18 minutes or until light golden brown or toothpick poked in center comes out clean.

Cool 5 minutes.

Loosen sides of muffins from pan if needed, and take them out of the pan.

33. Whole Wheat Honey Banana Muffins

Serves 24

What you'll need:

3 1/2 cups whole wheat flour
2 teaspoons baking soda
1 teaspoon salt
2 tablespoons wheat germ (optional)
2/3 cup olive oil or 2/3 cup canola oil
1 cup honey
4 eggs
2 cups mashed ripe bananas
1/2 cup hot water

What to do:

Stir together dry ingredients.

Beat oil and honey together; add eggs and beat well.

Add bananas and beat to combine.

Add dry ingredients to wet, alternating with hot water; mix well after each addition.

Spoon batter into 24 greased muffin cups; bake at 325 degrees for 15 minutes, or until muffins are golden brown and test done.

Remove from oven and cool on rack.

34. Double Chocolate Banana Muffins

Serves 12

What you'll need:

1 1/2 cups flour
1 cup sugar
1/4 cup baking cocoa
1 teaspoon baking soda
1/2 teaspoon salt
1/4 teaspoon baking powder
1 1/3 cups mashed ripe bananas
1/3 cup vegetable oil
1 egg
1 cup miniature semisweet chocolate chips

What to do:

In a large bowl, combine the first six ingredients.

In a small bowl, combine bananas, oil and egg.

Stir into dry ingredients just until moistened.

Fold in chocolate chips.

Fill greased or paper lined muffin cups three fourths full.

Bake at 350 F for 20-25 minutes.

35. Pecan Pie Muffins

Serves 4

What you'll need:

1 cup pecans, chopped
1 cup brown sugar, firmly packed
1/2 cup flour
2 large eggs
1/2 cup butter, melted

What to do:

Combine first 3 ingredients in a large bowl, make a well in center of mixture.

Beat eggs until foamy.

Stir together eggs and butter; add to dry ingredients stirring until moistened.

Place foil-baking cups in muffin pans.

Spoon batter into cups to 2/3 full.

Bake at 350 F for 20-25 minutes or until done.

Remove from pans immediately, cool on wire racks.

Best served warm.

36. Raspberry Corn Muffins

Serves 12

What you'll need:

Standard 12-cup muffin pan
1 cup cornmeal
1 1/4 cups unbleached all-purpose flour
1/2 cup granulated sugar
2 teaspoons baking powder
1 1/2 teaspoons baking soda
1/2 teaspoon kosher salt
2 large eggs
3/4 cup buttermilk or 3/4 cup whole milk mixed with 1 teaspoon lemon juice
12 tablespoons (1 1/2 sticks) unsalted butter, melted
3 tablespoons honey
1 1/2 cups raspberries

What to do:

Preheat the oven to 400°F. Grease the cups of a muffin pan with nonstick cooking spray or butter or fill with paper liners.

In a medium bowl, stir the cornmeal with the flour, sugar, baking powder, baking soda, and salt.

In another medium bowl, whisk the eggs and buttermilk, then whisk in the butter and honey. Using a rubber spatula or large spoon, stir in the flour mixture until the batter is evenly combined and no dry streaks are visible. Add the raspberries and gently mix until everything is barely blended—to keep the muffins light don't overmix the batter.

Spoon the batter into the prepared muffin cups, filling them equally. Bake until a bamboo skewer or toothpick inserted into the middles of the muffins comes out clean and the tops are golden brown, about 20 minutes. Let cool in the pan for 5 minutes and then use a small paring knife to pop them out of the cups.

37. Molasses Muffins with Flax and Dates

Serves 12

What you'll need:

1 egg (or substitute) or 2 egg whites
1/3 cup molasses
1 cup buttermilk (or 1 cup milk mixed with 1 teaspoon vinegar)
3/4 cup ground flaxseed meal
1/2 teaspoon salt
1 cup chopped dates
1 1/2 cups flour, preferably half whole wheat and half white
1 teaspoon baking soda

Optional: 1/2 teaspoon cinnamon; 1 teaspoon grated orange rind; 1 teaspoon vanilla extract

What to do:

Preheat the oven to 350 F, and prepare 12 muffin cups with papers or cooking spray.

In a large bowl, mix together the egg, molasses, buttermilk, flax, and salt, and add the dates to the batter.

In a separate bowl, mix together the flour and baking soda (and cinnamon).

Gently stir the flour mixture (and orange rind and vanilla) into the egg mixture.

Fill the muffin cups 2/3 full. Bake for 18 to 20 minutes or until a toothpick inserted near the center comes out clean.

38. Date Muffins

Serves 12

What you'll need:

For the Streusel Topping:

2 tablespoons flour
3 tablespoons rolled oats
1/4 cup packed brown sugar
1/2 cup chopped toasted pecans
2 tablespoons unsalted butter, softened

For the Muffins:

9 ounces whole Medjool dates, pitted (about 14 dates or 2 cups)
3/4 cup boiling water
2 cups flour
2 1/2 teaspoons baking powder
1/2 teaspoon salt
4 tablespoons (1/2 stick) unsalted butter, softened
3/4 cup packed dark brown sugar
2 eggs
1 teaspoon vanilla

What to do:

To make the streusel topping:
In a medium bowl, stir together the flour, oats, brown sugar, and pecans. Using a fork, cut in butter until well combined and mixture begins to hold together a bit. Set aside.

To make the muffins:
Preheat the oven to 375°F. Butter a 12-cup muffin tin. Place the dates in a shallow bowl (in a single layer if possible), pour the boiling

water over them, and soak for 15 minutes. Transfer the dates and soaking liquid to a food processor and puree until almost smooth but a few pea-sized fruit pieces remain. Set aside to cool slightly.

In a medium bowl, combine the flour, baking powder, and salt. Set aside.

In the bowl of an electric mixer, cream together the butter and brown sugar. With the motor running, mix in the eggs, one at a time. Add the vanilla. Add half of the flour mixture and mix until moistened. Follow with the date puree, and when thoroughly combined, mix in remainder of the flour mixture. Scrape down the sides and give a final stir with a spatula to make sure all ingredients are thoroughly combined. Divide the batter among the muffin cups. Top with the streusel and press down gently to adhere. Bake for 20 to 25 minutes.

39. Cranberry Pecan Streusel Muffins

Serves 12

What you'll need:

Topping:

2 tablespoons all-purpose flour
2 tablespoons granulated sugar
Pinch of salt
1/4 teaspoon ground cinnamon
1 tablespoon unsalted butter, cut up
1/4 cup (1 ounce) pecans or walnuts, finely chopped

Muffins:

1/2 cup granulated sugar
1 cup cranberries, coarsely chopped
1/2 cup (2 ounces) pecans or walnuts, chopped
1 teaspoon grated orange zest
1 teaspoon orange extract
1 large egg at room temperature
1 cup plain or orange yogurt, top liquid poured off
4 tablespoons (1/4 cup) unsalted butter, melted, or canola oil
2 tablespoons wheat germ
1 1/2 cups unsifted all-purpose flour
2 teaspoons baking powder
1/2 teaspoon baking soda, if using
1/2 teaspoon salt
1/2 teaspoon cinnamon

What to do:

Position rack in center of the oven. Preheat oven to 400°F and bake 20 to 22 minutes. Prepare the pan as directed.

In a medium bowl, toss together all streusel topping ingredients and pinch everything together with your fingertips to make crumbs. Set aside.

Measure the sugar. In another bowl, toss together the cranberries and nuts with the grated orange zest, extract, and 1 tablespoon of sugar. Set aside.

In a large bowl, whisk together the egg(s), yogurt or milk, melted butter or oil, the remaining sugar, and the wheat germ. Place a sifter over the bowl and measure the flour, baking powder, baking soda (if using), salt, and cinnamon into it. Stir/sift the dry ingredients onto the wet, add the cranberry-nut mixture, and stir everything together just to blend; don't over-beat.

Divide the batter evenly among the muffin cups, filling them nearly full. Sprinkle generously with the streusel crumbs. (Half-fill any empty cups with water.) Bake 20 to 22 minutes (or for the time indicated for your altitude in the chart), or until the muffins are golden brown and well risen and a cake tester inserted in the center comes out clean. Cool slightly on a wire rack, and serve warm.

40. Cornbread Muffins with Maple Butter

Serves 12

What you'll need:

Maple butter:

3/4 cup (1 1/2 sticks) unsalted butter, room temperature
3 1/2 tablespoons pure maple syrup (preferably grade B)

Muffins:

1 cup yellow cornmeal
1 cup unbleached all-purpose flour
1/4 cup sugar
1 tablespoon baking powder
1/4 teaspoon salt
1 cup buttermilk
1 large egg
5 tablespoons unsalted butter, melted, cooled slightly

What to do:

For maple butter:
Using electric mixer, beat butter in medium bowl until creamy.
Gradually beat in maple syrup until well blended and smooth.

For muffins:
Preheat oven to 375°F. Butter 12 regular (1/3-cup) muffin cups. Sift
cornmeal, flour, sugar, baking powder, and salt into medium bowl.
Whisk buttermilk and egg in another medium bowl; whisk in melted
butter. Add buttermilk mixture to dry ingredients; stir just until
incorporated (do not overmix). Divide batter equally among prepared
muffin cups.

Bake muffins until tester inserted into center comes out clean, about 15 minutes (muffins will be pale). Cool on rack 10 minutes. Serve with maple butter.

41. Mocha Muffins

Serves 12

What you'll need:

1 egg
2 egg whites
1/2 cup milk
1 tablespoon instant coffee powder
1 tablespoon water
2 teaspoons vanilla extract
1 1/2 cups all-purpose flour
1/2 cup malted milk powder
1/2 cup white sugar
2 teaspoons baking powder
1/2 teaspoon salt
1/2 teaspoon ground cinnamon
2 tablespoons white sugar

What to do:

Preheat oven to 400 degrees F (205 degrees C). Grease muffin cups.

Mix together egg, egg whites, and milk. Stir in coffee powder, water, and vanilla.

In a large bowl, mix together flour, malted milk powder, 1/2 cup sugar, baking powder, and salt. Stir in liquid mixture. Mix together really well, until batter is thin and gooey like cake batter. Fill muffin cups 2/3 full. In a small bowl, stir together cinnamon and 2 tablespoons sugar. Sprinkle cinnamon sugar over muffins.

Bake in preheated oven for 20 to 25 minutes.

42. Multigrain Muffins

Serves 8

What you'll need:

1/3 cup whole wheat flour
1/3 cup soy flour
1/3 cup rye flour
1 teaspoon baking powder
1 teaspoon baking soda
1/2 teaspoon salt
1 tablespoon vegetable oil
1 egg, beaten
1 cup buttermilk
1 tablespoon molasses

What to do:

Preheat oven to 450 degrees F (230 degrees C). Lightly grease 8 muffin cups.

In a large bowl, mix together whole wheat flour, soy flour, rye flour, baking powder, baking soda, and salt. Work in oil with fingers, pastry blender or a fork. Add egg, buttermilk and molasses; stir well. Scoop into prepared muffin cups.

Bake in preheated oven for 17 minutes, or until a toothpick inserted into the center of a muffin comes out clean.

43. Fruit Muffins

Serves 12

What you'll need:

2 cups all-purpose flour
3 teaspoons baking powder
1/2 teaspoon salt
1/2 cup white sugar
1/4 cup shortening
1 cup milk
1 cup apple - peeled, cored and chopped

What to do:

Preheat oven to 400 degrees F (200 degrees C). Lightly grease 12 muffin cups.

In a large bowl, sift together the flour, baking powder and salt.

In a separate bowl, cream together sugar and shortening. Stir the flour mixture into the sugar mixture alternately with the milk. Fold in the fruit. Pour batter into prepared muffin pans.

Bake in preheated oven for 20 to 25 minutes, until a toothpick inserted into the center of a muffin comes out clean.

44. Mulberry Muffins

Serves 8

What you'll need:

1 1/2 cups all-purpose flour
1/2 cup white sugar
1 teaspoon baking powder
1/2 teaspoon baking soda
1 pinch salt
1/2 cup fat free sour cream
1/4 cup skim milk
2 tablespoons applesauce
1 egg
1/2 teaspoon almond extract
1/2 cup mulberries

What to do:

Preheat oven to 400 degrees F (200 degrees C).Grease 6 jumbo muffin cups or line with paper muffin liners.

Combine flour, sugar, baking powder, soda and salt. In a medium bowl, mix together sour cream, milk, applesauce, egg and almond extract. Stir in flour mixture until batter is smooth. Fold in mulberries. Spoon batter into prepared muffin cups.

Bake in preheated oven for 25 to 30 minutes, until a toothpick inserted into center of a muffin comes out clean.

45. Sprinkles Muffins

Serves 6

What you'll need:

1/4 cup butter
1/4 cup white sugar
1 egg
1 teaspoon vanilla extract
1/2 cup milk
1/4 cup strawberry flavored yogurt
1 1/2 cups self-rising flour
1/4 cup white chocolate chips
1/4 cup multicolored candy sprinkles

What to do:

Preheat the oven to 375 degrees F (190 degrees C). Grease a muffin tin, or line with paper liners.

In a medium bowl, cream together the butter and sugar until light and fluffy. Beat in the egg and vanilla, then gradually stir in the milk and yogurt. Add the flour, and mix until just blended. Fold in the white chocolate chips and sprinkles. Spoon into 6 muffin cups.

Bake for 15 to 20 minutes in the preheated oven, or until the tops spring back when lightly touched. Cool muffins before removing from the tin.

46. Blackberry Muffins

Serves 12

What you'll need:

1 cup milk
1 egg
3 tablespoons butter, melted
1 teaspoon vanilla extract
2 cups all-purpose flour
1 cup rolled oats
1 cup packed dark brown sugar
1 1/2 teaspoons baking powder
1/2 teaspoon baking soda
1/2 teaspoon pumpkin pie spice
1/2 teaspoon salt
1 1/2 cups fresh blackberries
1/4 cup turbinado raw sugar

What to do:

Preheat an oven to 400 degrees F (200 degrees C). Grease 12 muffin cups, or line with paper muffin liners. Whisk the milk, egg, butter, and vanilla extract together in a bowl.

Mix the flour, oats, brown sugar, baking powder, baking soda, pumpkin pie spice, and salt in a bowl. Make a well in the center and pour in the egg mixture. Stir until just combined. Gently fold in the blackberries. Divide the batter evenly into the muffin cups, and sprinkle with the turbinado sugar.

Bake in the preheated oven until a toothpick inserted into the center of a muffin comes out clean, about 20 minutes. Cool in the pans for

10 minutes before removing to cool completely on a wire rack.

47. Calypso Muffins

Serves 12

What you'll need:

1 cup water
1/2 cup rolled oats
1 1/2 cups all-purpose flour
1/4 cup wheat bran
1/3 cup white sugar
4 teaspoons baking powder
1/8 teaspoon ground nutmeg
1 mashed banana
1 beaten egg
1 (8 ounce) can crushed pineapple, well drained
1 cup coconut milk
1/8 teaspoon coconut extract

What to do:

In a saucepan, bring water to a boil. stir in oats, and cook 1 minute. Cover, and remove from heat; allow to cool.

Preheat oven to 375 degrees F (190 degrees C). Grease and flour a muffin pan, or use paper liners.

In a large bowl, combine flour, bran, sugar, baking powder, and nutmeg. Make a well in the center, and add mashed banana, cooked and cooled oatmeal, egg, pineapple, coconut milk, and coconut extract. Mix until smooth. Scoop into 12 muffin cups.

Bake in preheated oven for 25 to 30 minutes, or until golden brown, and tops spring back when lightly tapped.

48. Cheddar Muffins

Serves 12

What you'll need:

2 cups all-purpose flour
3 1/2 teaspoons baking powder
1 teaspoon salt
1 teaspoon paprika
1/4 cup butter
1 egg
1 cup milk
1 cup shredded Cheddar cheese
2/3 cup raisins

What to do:

Sift flour with baking powder, salt, and paprika. Cut in butter finely. Stir in remaining ingredients just until dry ingredients are moistened.

Spoon into well-greased muffin pans. Bake in a preheated 425 degree F (220 degrees C) oven for 25 minutes.

49. Meatloaf Muffins

Serves 12

What you'll need:

2 pounds lean ground beef
1 (10.5 ounce) can condensed vegetable soup
1/2 cup chopped onion
1 cup dry bread crumbs
2 eggs
1 teaspoon salt
1 pinch ground black pepper
3/4 cup ketchup (optional)

What to do:

Preheat an oven to 350 degrees F (175 degrees C). Lightly grease a 12 cup muffin pan.

Mix ground beef, soup, onion, bread crumbs, eggs, salt, and pepper in a bowl. Scoop mixture evenly into prepared muffin cups.

Bake 1 hour in the preheated oven to a minimum temperature of 160 degrees F (70 degrees C). If desired, remove from oven after 50 minutes, drizzle ketchup on the top of each muffin, and return to oven for an additional 10 minutes.

50. Maple Muffins

Serves 12

What you'll need:

1 1/2 cups all-purpose flour
1/4 cup white sugar
2 teaspoons baking powder
1/2 teaspoon salt
1/4 cup shortening
1/4 cup rolled oats
1 egg, beaten
1/2 cup milk
1/2 cup real maple syrup

What to do:

Preheat oven to 400 degrees F (205 degrees C). Grease the cups of a 12-cup muffin pan.

Sift together flour, sugar, baking powder and salt. Cut in shortening until mixture resembles coarse crumbs. Stir in oats. Add egg, milk, and syrup. Stir only until dry ingredients are moistened. Fill greased muffin tins 3/4 full.

Bake for 18 to 20 minutes. Remove from oven, and let stand a few minutes before removing muffins from the pan.

51. Pizza Muffins

Serves 12

What you'll need:

2 1/2 cups all-purpose flour
2 teaspoons baking powder
1/2 teaspoon baking soda
1/2 teaspoon salt
1 teaspoon dried basil leaves
1/2 teaspoon dried oregano
2 tablespoons white sugar
3 sun-dried tomatoes packed in oil, drained and diced
2 1/2 cups shredded sharp Cheddar cheese, divided
4 green onions, chopped
1 egg, beaten
1 1/2 cups buttermilk

What to do:

Preheat oven to 375 degrees F (190 degrees C). Grease muffin cups or line with paper muffin liners.

In a large bowl, combine flour, baking powder, baking soda, salt, basil, oregano and sugar into large bowl; stir until well blended. Mix in tomatoes, 1.5 cups of cheese and onions. In another bowl beat egg, whisk in buttermilk and stir until combined. Spoon batter into muffin tins until half full. Sprinkle remaining 1 cup cheese on top of muffins.

Bake in preheated oven for 15 to 20 minutes, until a toothpick inserted into center of the muffin comes out clean.

52. Peach Muffins

Serves 16

What you'll need:

3 cups all-purpose flour
1 tablespoon ground cinnamon
1 teaspoon baking soda
1 teaspoon salt
1 1/4 cups vegetable oil
3 eggs, lightly beaten
2 cups white sugar
2 cups peeled, pitted, and chopped peaches

What to do:

Preheat oven to 400 degrees F (200 degrees C). Lightly grease 16 muffin cups.

In a large bowl, mix the flour, cinnamon, baking soda, and salt. In a separate bowl, mix the oil, eggs, and sugar. Stir the oil mixture into the flour mixture just until moist. Fold in the peaches. Spoon into the prepared muffin cups.

Bake 25 minutes in the preheated oven, until a toothpick inserted in the center of a muffin comes out clean. Cool 10 minutes before turning out onto wire racks to cool completely.

53. Orange Muffins

Serves 12

What you'll need:

2 cups all-purpose flour
2 teaspoons baking powder
1/4 teaspoon baking soda
1 teaspoon salt
1/2 cup white sugar
1 tablespoon grated orange zest
2/3 cup orange juice
1/2 cup melted butter
2 eggs
1/2 cup ground walnuts (optional)
1 tablespoon melted butter
1/4 cup packed brown sugar
1/2 teaspoon ground cinnamon

What to do:

Combine flour, baking powder, baking soda, salt, white sugar and grated orange peel. Stir in orange juice, 1/2 cup melted butter, eggs and chopped nuts.

Pour into 12 muffin cups.

Blend 1 tablespoon melted margarine, 1/4 cup brown sugar, 1/2 teaspoon cinnamon and sprinkle on top of each muffin. Bake in a preheated 350 degrees F (175 degrees C) oven for 20-25 minutes. Serve hot.

54. Coconut Key Lime Muffins

Serves 12

What you'll need:

1 1/2 cups (7 1/2 ounces) all-purpose flour
1 1/2 teaspoons baking powder
1/2 teaspoon baking soda
1/2 teaspoon salt
8 tablespoons unsalted butter, melted
1 cup (7 ounces) sugar
2/3 cup whole Greek yogurt
2 eggs
1 teaspoon zest and 1 tablespoon juice (from about 3 small key limes)
3/4 cup sweetened coconut flakes

What to do:

Adjust oven rack to middle position and preheat oven to 350°F. Line 12 muffin cups with paper holders. In a medium bowl, whisk together flour, baking powder, baking soda, and salt until combined; set aside.

In a large bowl, beat together butter and sugar with an electric beater until combined. Beat in yogurt, eggs, zest, and juice. Add dry ingredients and stir with a wooden spoon until evenly distributed.

Fill muffin tins 2/3 full with batter. Top each tin with coconut. Bake until a tester inserted into the center of a muffin comes about clean, about 20 minutes. Let cool for 5 minutes then transfer to a wire rack to finish cooling.

55. Blackberry Crumb Muffins

Serves 16

What you'll need:

2 cups flour
1 cup sugar
1/4 teaspoon baking soda
2 1/2 teaspoons baking powder
1/4 teaspoon salt
1 stick (8 tablespoons) unsalted butter, melted
2 large eggs
1 cup milk
12 ounces blackberries

For Crumb Topping:

1 stick (8 tablespoons) cold unsalted butter, cut into 1/4 inch pieces
3/4 cup all-purpose flour
3/4 cup packed dark brown sugar
1 teaspoon cinnamon
1/2 teaspoon salt

What to do:

Preheat oven to 400 degrees. Grease or line 16 muffin cups.

In a medium bowl, whisk together flour, sugar, baking powder, baking soda, and salt.

In a large bowl, whisk together butter, eggs, and milk. Add flour mixture to butter mixture and stir until just incorporated. Add blackberries and stir until evenly distributed.

Pour batter into prepared muffin tins, filling each cup 3/4 way full.

Make Crumb Topping: In a small bowl, combine butter, flour, dark brown sugar, cinnamon and salt. Use your hands to rub ingredients together until they are evenly blended together. Butter will be the size of peas, and flour will have been completely incorporated.

Top each muffin cup with crumb mixture. Bake muffins until a cake tester comes out clean, about 15 minutes.

56. Chocolate Coconut Muffins

Serves 10

What you'll need:

1 1/4 cups all-purpose flour
1 1/2 teaspoons baking powder
Pinch of salt
3/4 cup shredded coconut, divided
1/3 cup sugar
1/2 cup chocolate chips (or chopped chocolate)
1/2 cup butter, melted
1 cup milk
1 egg, beaten
1/2 teaspoon vanilla

What to do:

Preheat oven to 375 . In a mixing bowl combine flour, baking powder, salt, 1/2 cup shredded coconut and sugar and mix until combined then toss chocolate with dry ingredients until evenly distributed. In a separate bowl combine melted butter, milk, egg and vanilla and beat until well combined. Fold wet ingredients into dry ingredients with a rubber spatula, mixing until just combined (some lumps are ok).

Line muffin tin with 10 liners then divide batter between lined cups. Sprinkle each muffin with remaining shredded coconut and bake until muffins are puffed and coconut is brown, about 30 minutes. Remove from oven and allow to cool for 10 minutes before removing. Serve warm.

57. Bacon Cheese Muffins

Serves 12

What you'll need:

2 cups all-purpose flour
1 cup (4 ounces) shredded cheddar cheese
8 bacon strips, cooked and crumbled
2 tablespoons sugar
3 teaspoons baking powder
1/4 teaspoon salt
1/8 teaspoon garlic powder
1/8 teaspoon lemon-pepper seasoning
1 egg
1 cup milk
1/4 cup vegetable oil

What to do:

In a large bowl, combine the first eight ingredients. In another bowl, beat the egg, milk and oil. Stir into dry ingredients just until moistened.

Fill greased muffin cups two-thirds full. Bake at 400 F for 15-20 minutes or until a toothpick comes out clean. Cool for 5 minutes before removing from pan to a wire rack. Serve warm. Refrigerate leftovers.

58. Espresso Chocolate Muffins

Serves 12

What you'll need:

2 cups (10 ounces) all-purpose flour
1/2 cup (1 1/2 ounces) cocoa powder
2 teaspoons baking powder
1/2 teaspoon baking soda
1/2 teaspoon salt
3/4 cup (5 1/4 ounces) granulated sugar
2 large eggs
1/3 cup vegetable oil
1 cup plus 2 tablespoons milk
1 teaspoon pure vanilla extract
1 tablespoon espresso powder
1 1/2 cups chocolate chips, divided

What to do:

Adjust oven rack to middle position and preheat oven to 375 F. Spray standard muffin tin with non-stick pan spray. Sift flour, cocoa, baking powder, baking soda, and salt into medium bowl; set aside. In large bowl, whisk sugar with eggs until light, about 30 seconds. Whisk in oil, milk, vanilla, and espresso until combined.

Whisk dry mixture into wet mixture until just combined. Stir in 1 cup chips.

Evenly divide batter between muffin cups and sprinkle with remaining chips. Bake until set, 17 to 19 minutes. Let muffins cool in pan 15 minutes, then remove muffins from tin and place on wire rack to cool.

59. Banana Honey-Walnut Muffins

Serves 12

What you'll need:

3/4 cup chopped walnuts
1/3 cup plus 1 tablespoon honey, divided
1/2 teaspoon cinnamon
1-1/2 cups all-purpose flour, spooned into measuring cup
1-1/2 teaspoons baking powder
1/2 teaspoon salt
1 stick unsalted butter, at room temperature
2/3 cup sugar
2 large eggs
1/2 cup mashed banana, from 1 large overripe banana
1 teaspoon vanilla extract
1/3 cup whole or low fat milk

What to do:

Preheat the oven to 350°. Spray a 12-cup muffin tin with non-stick cooking spray, then line with paper liners (you need to do both so that the muffin tops don't stick to pan).

In a small bowl, toss the nuts with 1 tablespoon of the honey and cinnamon until the nuts are evenly coated (will be very sticky). Set aside.

In a medium bowl, whisk together the flour, baking powder and salt. Set aside.

In a large bowl, using an electric mixer, beat the butter with the sugar and the remaining 1/3 cup of honey until fluffy, 2-3 minutes. Scrape down the sides of the bowl with a rubber spatula if necessary. At medium speed, add the eggs one at a time and beat until fully incorporated between additions. Beat in the banana and vanilla until blended. At low speed, beat in the dry ingredients in 2 batches, alternating with the milk.

Spoon the batter into the prepared muffin tin and sprinkle with the nut topping. Bake the muffins until the tops are golden and a toothpick inserted in the center comes out clean, about 30 minutes. Let the muffins cool in the pan for 10 minutes, then turn them out onto a rack and let cool for at least 15 minutes before serving.

60. Orange Marmalade Muffins

Serves 12

What you'll need:

2 cups flour
2/3 cup sugar
2 teaspoons baking powder
1/4 teaspoon baking soda
1 teaspoon salt
2/3 cup orange juice
1/2 cup safflower oil (or other neutral oil)
2 eggs
1/4 cup orange marmalade
2 tablespoons chopped walnuts (optional)

What to do:

Preheat the oven to 350 F. Place liners in 12 muffin cups, or grease them well.

In a small mixing bowl, combine the dry ingredients: flour, sugar, baking powder, baking soda, and salt.

In a larger mixing bowl, whisk together the orange juice, oil, eggs, and marmalade.

Sprinkle the dry ingredients over the wet ingredients, and fold to combine (a few lumps are OK, don't overmix)

Fill the muffin cups about 3/4 full, and top each with some walnuts if you're using them.

Bake for 20-25 minutes, until the muffins have risen, and they spring back when you put slight pressure on them. Test with a toothpick in the center of the muffin; if it comes out dry, it's done.

Serve warm.

61. Double Chocolate Chunk Muffins

Serves 12

What you'll need:

3/4 of a stick (6 tablespoons) unsalted butter
4 ounces bittersweet chocolate, coarsely chopped
2 cups all-purpose flour
2/3 cup sugar
1/3 cup unsweetened cocoa powder, sifted
1 tablespoon baking powder
1/2 teaspoon baking soda
1/2 teaspoon salt
1 1/4 cups buttermilk
1 large egg
2 teaspoon pure vanilla extract

What to do:

Center a rack in the oven and preheat the oven to 375 degrees F. Butter or spray the 12 molds in a regular-size muffin pan or fit the molds with paper muffin cups. Alternatively, use a silicone muffin pan, which needs neither greasing nor paper cups. Place the muffin pan on a baking sheet.

Melt the butter and half the chopped chocolate together in a bowl over a saucepan of simmering water; or do this in a microwave. Remove from the heat.

In a large bowl, whisk together the flour, sugar, cocoa, baking powder, baking soda and salt. In a large glass measuring cup or another bowl, whisk the buttermilk, egg and vanilla extract together until well combined. Pour the liquid ingredients and the melted butter and chocolate over the dry ingredients and, with the whisk or a rubber spatula, gently but quickly stir to blend. (Don't overmix). Stir in the remaining chopped chocolate. Divide the batter evenly among the muffin molds.

Bake for 20 minutes, or until a thin knife inserted into the center of the muffins comes out clean. Transfer the pan to a rack and cool 5 minutes before carefully removing each muffin from its mold.

62. Raspberry-Topped Lemon Muffins

Serves 14

What you'll need:

1 1/4 cups sugar, divided
4 teaspoons finely grated lemon peel
2 cups all-purpose flour
2 1/2 teaspoons baking powder
3/4 teaspoon salt
1/2 cup (1 stick) unsalted butter, room temperature
1 large egg
1 cup buttermilk
2 teaspoons vanilla extract
1 1/2 1/2-pint containers (about) fresh raspberries
1/4 cup (about) whipping cream

What to do:

Preheat oven to 375 F. Line 14 standard muffin cups with paper liners. Mash 1/4 cup sugar and lemon peel in small bowl until sugar is slightly moist. Whisk flour, baking powder, and salt in medium bowl to blend. Using electric mixer, beat remaining 1 cup sugar and butter in large bowl until smooth. Beat in egg. Beat in buttermilk, then vanilla and half of lemon sugar. Beat in flour mixture.

Divide batter among muffin cups. Top each muffin with 4 raspberries. Bake muffins until lightly browned on top and tester inserted into center comes out clean, about 35 minutes. Brush tops of muffins lightly with cream; sprinkle with remaining lemon sugar and cool.

63. Healthy Blueberry and Banana Muffins

Serves 12

What you'll need:

1 1/2 cups all-purpose flour
1/2 cup sugar
1/4 cup oat bran
2 teaspoons baking powder
1/2 teaspoon salt
1 cup mashed ripe bananas (about 3)
1/2 cup unflavored soy milk
1 large egg
2 tablespoons vegetable oil
2 teaspoons fresh lemon juice
1 1/2 cups fresh blueberries or frozen blueberries, unthawed (6 or 7 ounces)

What to do:

Preheat oven to 400 F. Line 12 muffin cups with paper liners. Combine flour, sugar, oat bran, baking powder, and salt in medium bowl; whisk to blend.

Place mashed bananas in large bowl. Stir in soy milk, egg, oil, and lemon juice. Mix in dry ingredients, then blueberries. Divide batter among muffin papers. Bake muffins until tester inserted into center comes out clean, about 20 minutes. Turn muffins out onto rack and cool 10 minutes. Serve warm or at room temperature.

64. Bacon Corn Muffins

Serves 12

What you'll need:

1 1/4 cups whole milk
1 large egg
3/4 stick (6 tablespoons) unsalted butter, melted and cooled
1 cup yellow cornmeal
3/4 cup all-purpose flour
1 cup chopped scallions
8 bacon slices, cooked and crumbled (1/2 pound)
2 tablespoons sugar
1 tablespoon baking powder
3/4 teaspoon salt

What to do:

Put oven rack in middle position and preheat oven to 400 F.

Whisk together milk, egg, and butter in a small bowl. Whisk together remaining ingredients in a large bowl, then add milk mixture to dry ingredients. Stir until just combined.

Divide among 12 greased (1/2-cup) muffin cups. Bake until golden and a tester comes out clean, about 20 minutes. Cool in pan on a rack 5 to 10 minutes.

65. Carrot Spice Muffins

Serves 18

What you'll need:

1 1/2 cups whole wheat flour
1 teaspoon baking soda
1 teaspoon baking powder
1/2 teaspoon salt (optional)
1/2 teaspoon cinnamon
1/4 teaspoon nutmeg
1/8 teaspoon ground ginger
1/8 teaspoon allspice
1/3 cup honey or 1/3 cup brown sugar
1 egg
1/2 cup buttermilk or 1/2 cup yogurt
1/3 cup oil or melted butter or applesauce
1/2 teaspoon vanilla
1 1/2 cups grated carrots
1/2 cup raisins
1/2 cup chopped nuts

What to do:

Preheat oven to 400 F.

Mix together dry ingredients- flour, soda, powder, salt, cinnamon, nutmeg, ginger, allspice.

Mix together wet ingredients- honey/brown sugar, egg, buttermilk/yogurt, oil, vanilla and the carrots, raisins and nuts.

Stir the wet and dry ingredients together until just moistened.

Bake for about 15 minutes, or until a toothpick inserted into the center of a muffin comes out clean.

66. Blueberry Buttermilk Muffins

Serves 12

What you'll need:

2 1/2 cups flour
1 1/2 teaspoons baking powder
1/2 teaspoon baking soda
3/4 cup sugar
1/4 teaspoon salt
2 eggs, beaten
1 cup buttermilk
4 ounces butter or 1/2 cup canola oil
1 1/2 cups blueberries
1 teaspoon vanilla (optional)

What to do:

Sift dry ingredients together in a large bowl.

In another bowl, whisk eggs, buttermilk and butter that has been melted and browned slightly.

Make a well in dry ingredients and pour in liquid ingredients, mixing quickly.

Fold in blueberries.

Spoon batter into greased muffin cups and bake till golden brown.

Bake at 400 F for 20 -30 minutes.

67. Cappuccino Muffins

Serves 14

What you'll need:

For the Spread:

4 ounces cream cheese, cubed
1 tablespoon sugar
1/2 teaspoon instant coffee granules
1/2 teaspoon vanilla extract
1/4 cup miniature semisweet chocolate chips

For the Muffins:

2 cups all-purpose flour
3/4 cup sugar
2 1/2 teaspoons baking powder
1 teaspoon cinnamon, ground
1/2 teaspoon salt
1 cup milk
2 tablespoons instant coffee granules
1/2 cup butter or 1/2 cup margarine, melted
1 egg, beaten
1 teaspoon vanilla extract
3/4 cup miniature semisweet chocolate chips

What to do:

In a food processor (or using a hand mixer), combine the spread ingredients, cover and process until well blended.

For the muffins: In a bowl, combine flour, sugar, baking powder, cinnamon and salt. In another bowl, stir milk and coffee granules until coffee is dissolved.

Add butter, egg and vanilla; mix well. Stir into dry ingredients just until moistened. Fold in chocolate chips. Fill greased or paper-lined muffin cups two-thirds full.

Bake at 375°F for 17-20 minutes or until muffins test done. Cool for 5 minutes before removing from pans to wire racks.

Serve with espresso spread.

68. Cranberry Orange Muffins

Serves 12

What you'll need:

2 cups   flour
3/4 cup sugar
1 teaspoon baking powder
1/2 teaspoon baking soda
1/2 teaspoon salt
1 cup cranberries
1 egg
3/4 cup orange juice
1/4 cup vegetable oil
1 teaspoon grated orange rind

What to do:

Combine dry ingredients.

Stir in cranberries.

Beat egg, orange juice, oil and orange rind.

Add to dry ingredients all at once.

Stir just to moisten.

Spoon into greased muffin cups and fill 3/4 full.

Spring tops lightly with a bit of sugar.

Bake 400F 15-20 minutes till lightly browned and firm to the touch.

69. Chocolate Brownie Muffins

Serves 12

What you'll need:

3/4 cup good quality baking cocoa
1 teaspoon baking powder (heaping)
3/4 cup butter or 3/4 cup margarine, melted
1/2 cup boiling water
1 tablespoon vanilla
1 1/4 cups sugar (or to taste)
2 eggs
1 1/3 cups all-purpose flour
1/4 teaspoon salt
1/2 cup mini chocolate chip (optional)
1/2 cup walnuts (optional)

What to do:

Set oven to 350 F. and line 12 muffin tins with paper liners.

In a medium bowl combine cocoa and baking powder; mix to combine. Add in boiling water; mix well with a wooden spoon to combine. Add in the melted butter and vanilla; mix well. Add in the sugar, mix well with a wooden spoon.

Stir in eggs with a wooden spoon; mix until combined. Mix the flour with salt; add in the chocolate mixture; mix well to combine (batter will be a bit on the thin side). Add/mix in mini chocolate chips or walnuts (or both).

Using an ice cream scoop fill each of the muffin tins almost to the top.

Bake for 25-30 minutes or until muffins are done, don't over bake. (might take a little longer, depending on how full the muffin tins are with the batter).

Cool, drizzle glaze over or frost with buttercream frosting.

70. Zucchini Nut Muffins

Serves 24

What you'll need:

3 eggs
1 cup oil
1 2/3 cups sugar
1/3 cup brown sugar
2 cups zucchini, grated
3 cups flour, sifted
1 teaspoon baking soda
1/4 teaspoon baking powder
3 teaspoons cinnamon
1 teaspoon salt
1/2 cup walnuts, chopped

What to do:

Beat the eggs until they are light and foamy.

Add the sugar, oil and zucchini.

Blend well with a spoon.

Mix the dry ingredients and add to the egg mixture; blend well.

Add the nuts, and spoon into greased muffin tins.

Bake at 325°F for 20 minutes.

71. Strawberry Muffins

Serves 8

What you'll need:

1/4 cup canola oil
1/2 cup milk
1 egg
1/2 teaspoon salt
2 teaspoons baking powder
1/2 cup white sugar
1 3/4 cups all-purpose flour
1 cup chopped strawberries

What to do:

Preheat oven to 375 degrees F (190 degrees C) oil an 8 cup muffin tin, or use paper liners.

In a small bowl, combine oil, milk, and egg. Beat lightly. In a large bowl, mix flour, salt, baking powder and sugar. Toss in chopped strawberries and stir to coat with flour. Pour in milk mixture and stir together.

Fill muffin cups. Bake at 375 degrees F (190 degrees C) for 25 minutes, or until the tops bounce back from the touch. Cool 10 minutes and remove from pans.

72. Apple Muffins

Serves 12

What you'll need:

2 cups all-purpose flour
1/2 cup white sugar
3 teaspoons baking powder
1/2 teaspoon salt
3/4 cup apple juice
1/3 cup vegetable oil
1 egg
1 teaspoon ground cinnamon
1 cup apples - peeled, cored and finely diced

What to do:

Heat oven to 400 degrees F (205 degrees C). Grease bottoms only of 12 muffin cups or line with baking cups.

In a medium bowl, combine flour, sugar, baking powder, cinnamon, and salt; mix well. In a small bowl, combine apple juice, oil, and egg; blend well. Add dry ingredients all at once; stir just until dry ingredients are moistened (batter will be lumpy.) Stir in chopped apples.

Fill cups 2/3 full. Bake for 18 to 22 minutes or until toothpick inserted in center comes out clean. Cool 1 minute before removing from pan. Serve warm.

73. Lemon Muffins

Serves 12

What you'll need:

2 cups all-purpose flour
1/2 cup white sugar
3 teaspoons baking powder
1 tablespoon grated lemon zest
1/2 teaspoon salt
3/4 cup milk
1/3 cup vegetable oil
1 egg

What to do:

Heat oven to 400 degrees F (205 degrees C). Grease bottoms only of 12 muffin cups or line with baking cups.

In a medium bowl, combine flour, sugar, baking powder, lemon zest and salt; mix well. In a small bowl, combine milk, oil and egg; blend well. Add dry ingredients all at once; stir just until dry ingredients are moistened (batter will be lumpy.)

Fill cups 2/3 full. Bake for 20 to 25 minutes or until toothpick inserted in center comes out clean. Cool 1 minute before removing from pan. Serve warm.

74. Morning Glory Muffins

Serves 18

What you'll need:

1 1/2 cups all-purpose flour
1/2 cup whole wheat flour
1 1/4 cups white sugar
1 tablespoon ground cinnamon
2 teaspoons baking powder
1/2 teaspoon baking soda
1/2 teaspoon salt
2 cups grated carrots
1 apple - peeled, cored, and chopped
1 cup raisins
1 egg
2 egg whites
1/2 cup apple butter
1/4 cup vegetable oil
1 tablespoon vanilla extract
2 tablespoons chopped walnuts
2 tablespoons toasted wheat germ

What to do:

Preheat oven to 375 degrees F (190 degrees C). Lightly oil 18 muffin cups, or coat with nonstick cooking spray.

In a medium bowl, whisk together eggs, egg whites, apple butter, oil and vanilla.

In a large bowl, stir together flours, sugar, cinnamon, baking powder, baking soda and salt. Stir in carrots, apples and raisins. Stir in apple butter mixture until just moistened. Spoon the batter into the prepared muffin cups, filling them about 3/4 full.

In a small bowl, combine walnuts and wheat germ; sprinkle over the muffin tops.

Bake at 375 degrees F (190 degrees C) for 15 to 20 minutes, or until the tops are golden and spring back when lightly pressed.

75. Nut Blueberry Muffins

Serves 12

What you'll need:

3/4 cup all-purpose flour
3/4 cup whole wheat flour
3/4 cup white sugar
1/4 cup oat bran
1/4 cup quick cooking oats
1/4 cup wheat germ
1 teaspoon baking powder
1 teaspoon baking soda
1/4 teaspoon salt
1 cup blueberries
1/2 cup chopped walnuts
1 banana, mashed
1 cup buttermilk
1 egg
1 tablespoon vegetable oil
1 teaspoon vanilla extract

What to do:

Preheat the oven to 350 degrees F (175 degrees C). Grease a 12 cup muffin pan, or line with paper muffin cups.

In a large bowl, stir together the all-purpose flour, whole wheat flour, sugar, oat bran, quick-cooking oats, wheat germ, baking powder, baking soda and salt. Gently stir in the blueberries and walnuts. In a separate bowl, mix together the mashed banana, buttermilk, egg, oil and vanilla. Pour the wet ingredients into the dry, and mix just until blended. Spoon into muffin cups, filling all the way to the top.

Bake for 15 to 18 minutes in the preheated oven, or until the tops of the muffins spring back when lightly touched.

76. Banana Bread Muffins

Serves 12

What you'll need:

1 cup white sugar
1/2 cup vegetable oil
1 egg
3 ripe bananas, mashed
1/4 cup chopped walnuts
2 cups all-purpose flour
1 teaspoon baking soda
1/2 teaspoon salt

What to do:

Preheat oven to 350 degrees F (175 degrees C). Place muffin cups in muffin tin, or grease with a little butter.

Mix sugar, oil, and egg until creamy and light yellow in a bowl. Add bananas and walnuts. Add flour, baking soda, and salt. Stir until completely smooth. Spoon the batter into the muffin tin.

Bake for 30 to 40 minutes, until toothpick poked in center muffin comes out clean.

77. Agave Cornbread Muffins

Serves 6

What you'll need:

1/2 cup cornmeal
1/2 cup whole-wheat pastry flour
1/2 teaspoon baking soda
1/2 teaspoon salt
1/2 cup applesauce
1/2 cup soy milk
1/4 cup agave nectar
2 tablespoons canola oil

What to do:

Preheat oven to 325 degrees F (165 degrees C). Lightly grease a muffin pan.

Combine the cornmeal, flour, baking soda, and salt in a large bowl; stir in the applesauce, soy milk, and agave nectar. Slowly add the oil while stirring. Pour the mixture into the muffin pan.

Bake in the preheated oven until a toothpick or small knife inserted in the crown of a muffin comes out clean, 15 to 20 minutes.

78. Zucchini Yogurt Multigrain Muffins

Serves 24

What you'll need:

1 1/2 cups all-purpose flour
3/4 cup whole wheat flour
3/4 cup oat flour
1 teaspoon salt
1 teaspoon baking soda
1 teaspoon baking powder
2 1/2 teaspoons ground cinnamon
1/4 teaspoon ground nutmeg
3 eggs
1/2 cup vegetable oil
1/2 cup unsweetened applesauce
1 cup plain yogurt
1 cup white sugar
3/4 cup honey
2 teaspoons vanilla extract
1 cup shredded zucchini
1 cup shredded carrots
1/2 cup chopped pecans (optional)
1/2 cup raisins (optional)

What to do:

Preheat oven to 400 degrees F (200 degrees C). Lightly grease 24 muffin cups.

In a bowl, sift together the all-purpose flour, whole wheat flour, oat flour, salt, baking powder, baking soda, cinnamon, and nutmeg. In a separate bowl, beat together eggs, vegetable oil, applesauce, yogurt, sugar, honey, and vanilla. Mix the flour mixture into the egg mixture. Fold in the zucchini, carrots, pecans, and raisins. Scoop into the prepared muffin cups.

Bake 18 to 20 minutes in the preheated oven, until a toothpick inserted in the center of a muffin comes out clean. Cool 10 minutes before transferring to wire racks to cool completely.

79. Monkey Bread Muffins

Serves 6

What you'll need:

1 teaspoon apple pie spice
1/4 cup white sugar
1 (12 ounce) can refrigerated biscuit dough, separated and cut into six pieces
1/2 cup brown sugar
3 tablespoons butter
1 teaspoon water

What to do:

Preheat an oven to 375 degrees F (190 degrees C). Butter 6 muffin cups or line with paper muffin liners.

Combine the apple pie spice and white sugar in a small bowl; roll the biscuit pieces in the mixture to coat. Divide the coated pieces between the prepared muffin cups.

Combine the brown sugar, butter, and water in a small saucepan over medium heat; bring to a boil, stirring continuously. Allow the mixture to boil until the sugar is completely dissolved, 2 to 3 minutes. Spoon the mixture over the biscuit pieces.

Bake in the preheated oven until golden, and the tops spring back when lightly pressed, 8 to 12 minutes.

80. Honey Bran Muffins

Serves 20

What you'll need:

2 cups pineapple juice
2 cups golden raisins
1 cup packed brown sugar
1/2 cup vegetable oil
1/2 cup honey
5 eggs, beaten
2 cups all-purpose flour
2 teaspoons baking soda
1 teaspoon salt
4 cups whole bran cereal

What to do:

In a small bowl, combine pineapple juice and raisins. Set aside.

In a medium bowl, combine flour, baking soda and salt. Stir in cereal. Set aside.

In a large mixing bowl, combine brown sugar, oil, honey, and eggs; mix well. Add cereal mixture, and mix well. Fold in the raisin mixture. Batter will be thin; it will thicken as it chills. Cover, and refrigerate for at least 3 hours or overnight.

Stir chilled batter. Fill greased or paper lined muffin cups 3/4 full.

Bake in a preheated 400 degree F (205 degree C) oven, for 20 to 25 minutes. Cool in pan 10 minutes before removing to a wire rack.

81. Double Chocolate Cherry Muffins

Serves 12

What you'll need:

2 1/3 cups all-purpose flour
1 1/4 cups white sugar
1/3 cup unsweetened cocoa powder
2 teaspoons baking powder
1 teaspoon baking soda
1/2 teaspoon salt
1 cup sour cream
1/2 cup milk
1/3 cup vegetable oil
2 eggs, beaten
1 teaspoon almond extract
1 1/2 cups fresh dark sweet cherries, pitted and chopped
1 cup miniature semisweet chocolate chips

What to do:

Preheat an oven to 400 degrees F (200 degrees C). Grease 12 jumbo (3 1/2-inch) muffin cups or line with paper baking cups.

Stir together the flour, sugar, cocoa powder, baking powder, baking soda, and salt in a separate large bowl, and make a well in the center; set aside. Whisk together the sour cream, milk, vegetable oil, eggs, and almond extract in a bowl until evenly blended. Pour the sour cream mixture into the well, then stir in the flour mixture until just combined. Fold in the cherries and chocolate chips. Spoon into prepared muffin cups, filling half full.

Bake until a toothpick inserted into centers comes out clean, about 20 to 25 minutes. Cool in pan on wire rack 5 minutes. Remove from pan and cool completely on wire rack. Store tightly covered at room temperature.

82. Hearty Breakfast Muffins

Serves 12

What you'll need:

2 carrots, shredded
2 bananas, mashed
1 zucchini, shredded
1/4 cup vegetable oil
1/4 cup yogurt
2 eggs
1 cup whole wheat flour
1 1/2 teaspoons baking soda
1/2 cup packed brown sugar
1/2 cup rolled oats
1/2 cup shredded coconut
1/2 cup chopped pecans
1/2 cup dried cherries
1 teaspoon ground cinnamon
1 teaspoon salt
1/2 teaspoon ground ginger

What to do:

Preheat oven to 375 degrees F (190 degrees C). Grease 12 muffin cups or line with paper liners.

Mix carrots, banana, zucchini, vegetable oil, yogurt, and eggs together until fully incorporated.

Whisk flour and baking soda in a separate bowl. Mix brown sugar, oats, coconut, pecans, cherries, cinnamon, salt, and ginger into flour mixture until all ingredients are coated in flour. Stir wet ingredients into flour mixture until just combined. Scoop batter into the prepared muffin cups.

Bake in the preheated oven until a toothpick inserted in the center of a muffin comes out clean and edges are slightly brown, 17 to 22 minutes. Cool in the pans for 10 minutes before removing to cool completely on a wire rack.

83. Pumpkin Cream Cheese Muffins

Serves 24

What you'll need:

3 cups all-purpose flour
1 teaspoon cinnamon
1 teaspoon nutmeg
1 teaspoon ground cloves
4 teaspoons pumpkin pie spice
1 pinch cardamom (optional)
1 teaspoon salt
1 teaspoon baking soda
5 eggs
2 cups sugar and 3 tablespoons sugar
2 cups pumpkin
1 1/4 cups vegetable oil
8 ounces cream cheese
Chopped pumpkin seeds or walnuts or pecans (optional)

What to do:

Preheat oven to 350.

Mix cream cheese with one egg and 3 tablespoons of sugar. Put the entire mixture on a piece of wax paper or parchment paper and shape it into a long log.

Put it in the freezer while you mix and fill the pans, up to an hour.

Unwrap and cut with a sharp knife so each cream cheese disk equals 1-2 teaspoons. If the cream cheese disks are too big around, cut thick slices and then cut them in half. This lets you push it down into the batter easier.

Mix all ingredients together (except cream cheese and nuts). Fill muffin tins (greased or paper cups) half full. Put cream cheese disc in the middle, pressing down. Sprinkle with 1 tsp chopped nuts.

Bake at 350 for 20-25 minutes, until a toothpick comes out clean from the muffin part (do not touch the cream cheese!).

Let cool in pans for 5 minutes, then remove to racks to cool completely.

84. Corn Dog Muffins

Serves 18

What you'll need:

2 (8 1/2 ounce) packages cornbread mix
2 tablespoons brown sugar
2 eggs
1 cup milk
1 (11 ounce) can whole kernel corn, drained
5 hot dogs, chopped
1 cup cheddar cheese, shredded

What to do:

Combine mix and brown sugar, add eggs and milk stirring only until moistened.

Stir in drained corn, hot dogs, and cheese. Batter will be thin.

Fill paper lined muffin cups 2/3 full.

Bake at 400 degrees for 15 minutes or until tops are brown.

Serve immediately or refrigerate.

85. Scrambled Egg Muffins

Serves 12

What you'll need:

1/2 lb pork sausage
12 eggs
1/2 cup chopped onion
1/2 cup chopped green pepper
1/2 teaspoon salt
1/4 teaspoon pepper
1/4 teaspoon garlic powder
1/2 cup shredded sharp cheddar cheese

What to do:

Brown sausage; drain well.

Preheat oven to 350 F.

In a bowl, beat eggs, then add onion, green peppers, salt, pepper and garlic powder.

Stir in sausage and cheese.

Spoon 1/3 cupfuls into greased muffin cups.

Bake at 350° for 20-25 minutes or until a knife inserted comes out clean.

86. Baklava Muffins

Serves 12

What you'll need:

For the Filling:

1/2 cup walnuts, chopped
1/3 cup sugar
1 1/2 teaspoons cinnamon
3 tablespoons butter, melted

For the Muffins:

1 cup flour
7 tablespoons flour
2 teaspoons baking powder
1/2 teaspoon baking soda
1/4 cup sugar
1 large egg
3 tablespoons unsalted butter, melted
1 cup buttermilk
2 tablespoons buttermilk

For the Topping:

1/2 cup honey

What to do:

Preheat oven to 400 F degrees. Mix all the filling ingredients together in a small bowl, set aside.

In a large bowl, mix together the flour, baking powder, baking soda and sugar. Mix the egg, melted butter and buttermilk.

Make a well in the dry ingredients and add gently mix in the wet ingredients.

Fill 12 miffin cups 1/3 full, add a scant tablespoon of filling, cover with more muffin mixture until 2/3 full.

Sprinkle any remaining filling on top of the muffins. Bake for 15 minutes. Put the muffins onto a rack to cool and drizzle with honey.

87. Lemon Yogurt Muffins

Serves 12

What you'll need:

1 1/2 cups all-purpose flour
1 cup rolled oats
1/2 cup granulated sugar
2 teaspoons baking powder
1 teaspoon baking soda
1/2 teaspoon salt
1 1/4 cups plain yogurt
1 egg
1/4 cup lemon juice
1 lemon, peeled and chopped
1/4 cup granulated sugar
1/2 fresh lemon rind, peeled and chopped
1/2 lemon, juice of

What to do:

Preheat the oven to 400F (200C).

In a large bowl, mix together the flour, rolled oats, 1/2 cup granulated sugar, baking powder, baking soda and salt.

In a separate bowl, mix together the yogurt, egg, 1/4 cup lemon juice, and finely chopped peeled lemon (white pith removed first).

Add the wet ingredients to the dry, mixing only until blended.

Fill 12 well-greased muffin cups two thirds full. Bake for 20 minutes, or until a toothpick inserted into the centre of a muffin comes out clean.

Meanwhile, prepare the syrup: Put 1/4 cup granulated sugar and the grated rind and juice of 1/2 lemon in a small pot. Bring to a boil and reserve.

When the muffins are baked, prick all over with a toothpick.

Do not remove them from the pan until cooled. Brush the warm syrup on the hot muffins.

88. White Chocolate Raspberry Muffins

Serves 5

What you'll need:

1 cup milk
1/2 cup butter, melted
1 egg, slightly beaten
2 cups all-purpose flour
1/3 cup sugar
1 tablespoon baking powder
1 teaspoon salt
1 cup fresh raspberries or frozen raspberries (do not thaw)
1/2 cup vanilla chip

For the Muffin topping:

1/4 cup butter, melted
1/4 cup sugar

What to do:

Grease 12 muffin tin cups.

Heat oven to 400 F.

In a large bowl mix the milk, butter and egg.

Stir in all remaining muffin ingredients except raspberries & vanilla chips.

Stir only until flour is moistened, then gently stir in the berries & vanilla chips.

Spoon the batter into the greased muffin tins.

Bake for 24-28 minutes or until golden brown.

Let muffins cool a little, then remove from pan.

Dip top of each muffin top in melted butter, then in sugar.

89. Peach Nectarine Muffins

Serves 8

What you'll need:

1 1/2 cups flour
3/4 cup white sugar
1/2 teaspoon salt
2 teaspoons baking powder
1/3 cup vegetable oil
1 egg
1/3 cup milk
1 ripe peach (peeled, pitted, and diced)
1 ripe nectarine, pitted and diced (or use 1 1/2 cup other fruit)
1/8-1/4 cup brown sugar

What to do:

Preheat oven to 400 F.

Grease 8 muffin cups or use paper liners.

In a large bowl combine flour, white sugar, salt, and baking powder.

Add oil, egg, and milk.

Stir only until blended together.

Fold in fruit.

Fill muffin tins to the top.

Sprinkle tops with brown sugar.

Bake 15-20 minutes.

90. Garlic-Onion Muffins

Serves 12

What you'll need:

2 cups flour
3 teaspoons baking powder
1 teaspoon salt
2 tablespoons sugar
1 egg, beaten
1 cup milk
1/4 cup melted butter
2 garlic cloves, minced
1 medium onion, diced

What to do:

Heat oven to 400 F.

In a large bowl, mix flour, baking powder, salt and sugar.

In a small bowl, mix together egg, milk, garlic and onion.

Make a well in the center of dry ingredients and pour in the egg mixture and melted butter.

Mix together using as few strokes as possible.

Don't overmix, the batter should have small lumps in it.

Pour into 12 paper-lined muffins tins, filling about 2/3 full.

Bake 20 minutes or until muffins begin to turn golden on top.

Test for doneness with a toothpick which should come out clean.

Remove from tins and cool slightly before serving.

91. Lemonade Muffins

Serves 8

What you'll need:

1 1/2 cups flour
1/4 cup sugar
2 1/2 teaspoons baking powder
1/2 teaspoon salt
1 beaten egg
1 (6 ounce) can frozen lemonade, thawed
1/4 cup milk
1/3 cup cooking oil
1/2 cup chopped walnuts

What to do:

Mix dry ingredients in a bowl.

In another bowl, mix only 1/2 cup lemonade, egg, milk, and oil.

Add to dry mix, stirring until just moistened.

Gently stir in nuts.

Spoon into prepared pans and bake and bake at 375ºF. for 15-20 mins or tests clean.

While hot, brush with remaining lemonade and sprinkle with white sugar.

92. Yellow Squash Muffins

Serves 18

What you'll need:

2 lbs crookneck yellow squash
2 eggs
1/2 cup melted butter
1/2 cup applesauce
1 cup sugar
3 cups all-purpose flour
5 teaspoons baking powder
1 teaspoon salt

What to do:

Wash squash, trim ends, and cut into 1-inch slices.

Cook in a small amount of water for 15 to 20 minutes.

Drain well and mash.

Measure 2 cups of the cooked squash, combine with eggs, butter, and applesauce, and set aside.

Combine dry ingredients in a large bowl.

Make a well in center of mixture.

Add squash to dry ingredients, stirring only until moist.

Spoon into greased muffin tins, filling 3/4 full.

Bake at 375 degrees F for 20 minutes or until toothpick inserted in center of muffin comes out clean.

93. Banana Chocolate Chip Muffins

Serves 12

What you'll need:

1 1/2 cups flour
2/3 cup sugar
1 1/2 teaspoons baking powder
1/4 teaspoon salt
1 cup mashed banana
1 large egg
1/4 lb butter, melted
1/4 cup milk
3/4 cup chocolate chips

What to do:

Mix dry ingredients together.

Mix wet ingredients together.

Stir banana mixture gently into the dry ingredients till just moist.

Stir in chocolate chips.

Divide into 12 lined muffin cups and bake at 350°F about 30 minutes.

94. Pineapple Cream Muffins

Serves 15

What you'll need:

2 cups flour
2 teaspoons baking powder
1/2 teaspoon baking soda
1 (3 ounce) package vanilla instant pudding mix
2/3 cup brown sugar
1 egg, beaten
1 cup sour cream (can use low fat)
1 (8 ounce) can crushed pineapple in juice
1/2 cup oil

What to do:

Preheat oven to 425 F.

Spray muffin cups with nonstick spray or line with paper cupcake liners.

In a large bowl, sift together the flour, baking powder, baking soda and pudding mix, then stir in brown sugar.

In a separate bowl, combine the egg and sour cream.

Fold in the pineapple and oil.

Add the egg-pineapple mixture to the flour mixture and stir until moistened.

Batter will be thick.

Bake at 425 degrees for 15 minutes.

95. Whole Wheat Flax'n Apple Muffins

Serves 12

What you'll need:

1/4 cup ground flax seeds
3/4 cup whole wheat graham flour
3/4 cup white flour
1/2 cup sugar
2 teaspoons baking powder
1/2 teaspoon baking soda
1/2 teaspoon salt
1 egg, beaten
1 1/2 cups finely chopped apples
3 tablespoons canola oil
1/2 cup milk
1/2 cup chopped nuts

What to do:

Blend all dry ingredients together in a bowl.

In a separate bowl; combine egg, oil, and milk; add dry ingredients to egg mixture and stir until just blended. Don't overmix.

Fold in apples and nuts; batter will be thick.

Fill well-greased muffin cups 2/3 full; bake at 400 degrees for 18 to 20 minutes, or until tops spring back when touched.

96. Raspberry Buttermilk Muffins

Serves 12

What you'll need:

2 cups all-purpose flour
1/2 cup sugar
2 teaspoons baking powder
1 teaspoon salt
6 tablespoons butter
1 egg, beaten
1 cup buttermilk
1 cup fresh raspberry

What to do:

Combine flour, sugar, baking powder and salt.

Cut in butter until mixture resembles coarse crumbs.

Add egg and buttermilk; mix just until dry ingredients are moistened.

Fold in berries.

Fill greased or paper-lined muffin cups two-thirds full.

Bake at 400 F for 20 minutes or until browned.

97. Snickerdoodle Muffins

Serves 24

What you'll need:

For the Topping:

1/3 cup granulated sugar
1 teaspoon ground cinnamon

For the Muffins:

1 cup all-purpose flour
1/2 cup whole wheat flour
1 cup oats (quick or old fashioned, uncooked)
1/2 cup granulated sugar
1 tablespoon baking powder
1 cup nonfat milk
1 egg, lightly beaten
4 tablespoons margarine or 4 tablespoons butter, melted
1 teaspoon vanilla

What to do:

Heat oven to 400 F. Spray bottoms only of mini muffin pan cups with cooking spray.

For topping, combine sugar and cinnamon in small bowl; mix well and set aside.

For muffins, combine flour, oats, sugar and baking powder in large bowl; mix well. In small bowl, combine milk, egg, margarine and vanilla; blend well. Add to dry ingredients all at once; stir just until dry ingredients are moistened. (Don't overmix.)

Fill muffin cups two-thirds full. Sprinkle topping evenly over tops of muffins.

Bake 12 to 14 minutes or until light golden brown. Cool muffins in pan on wire rack 5 minutes; remove from pan. Serve warm.

98. Southern Biscuit Muffins

Serves 12

What you'll need:

2 1/2 cups all-purpose flour
3 tablespoons sugar
1 1/2 tablespoons baking powder
3/4 cup cold butter or 3/4 cup margarine
1 cup cold milk

What to do:

Preheat oven to 400 F.

Grease one 12-cup muffin pan (2 1/2-inch size).

In large bowl combine flour, sugar and baking powder.

Cut butter into thin slices and add to dry mixture.

Using a pastry cutter or low speed of your mixer, combine the butter with the dry mixture until it resembles coarse crumbs.

Stir in milk, with a spoon or fork.

Stirring only until flour mixture is moistened.

Batter will be thick and lumpy.

Spoon into muffin cups, dividing evenly between all 12 cups.

Bake for 20 minutes or until tops are golden brown.

When done, remove from muffin pan immediately.

99. Chocolate Cheesecake Muffins

Serves 8

What you'll need:

3 ounces cream cheese, softened
2 tablespoons sugar
1 cup flour
1/2 cup sugar
3 tablespoons cocoa powder
2 teaspoons baking powder
1/2 teaspoon salt
1 egg, beaten
3/4 cup milk
1/3 cup oil

What to do:

In a small bowl, beat cream cheese and 2 Tbsp sugar until light and fluffy.

Set aside.

In a large bowl, stir together flour, 1/2 cup sugar, cocoa, baking powder and salt.

Make a well in center of dry ingredients.

Combine egg, milk and oil.

Add all at once to dry ingredients stirring just until moistened.

(batter should be lumpy) Spoon about 2 Tbsp of batter into each greased muffin tray.

Drop 1 tsp of cream cheese mixture on top and then more of the chocolate batter.

Bake 375 F degrees for 20 minutes.

100. Mango Muffins

Serves 18

What you'll need:

2 cups flour
4 teaspoons baking powder
1/2 teaspoon salt
1 cup sugar or 3/4 cup honey
1/4 cup vegetable oil
1 cup milk
1 egg
1 -1 1/2 cup mango, pulp of (2 very ripe mangoes)

What to do:

Cut and peel two very ripe (soft to the touch) mangoes and reduce to soft pulp and juice. Combine flour, baking powder, salt and sugar in a large bowl.

In a separate bowl combine oil, milk, and egg.

Mix liquid ingredients with dry until just moist and stir in the mango pulp.

Fill greased muffin tins, or paper muffin cups two-thirds full.

Bake at 400 F for 15-18 minutes.

They are done when they are brown on top and a tooth-pick inserted into the center comes out clean.

101. Almond Poppy Seed Muffins

Serves 24

What you'll need:

3 cups flour
2 1/4 cups sugar
1 1/2 teaspoons baking powder
1 1/2 teaspoons salt
1 1/2 cups milk
1 1/2 cups vegetable oil
3 eggs
1/2-1 teaspoon almond extract
1 1/2 tablespoons poppy seeds

What to do:

Preheat oven to 350 F.

Grease, spray, or placed liners in muffin tins to hold 24 muffins.

Combine flour, sugar, baking powder and salt.

Add milk, eggs, oil, and almond extract; whisk until smooth but don't overmix.

Gently stir in poppy seeds.

Fill muffin tins and bake for 25- 30 minutes.

Thank You

Thank you so much for downloading my Muffin cookbook.
I really hope you had a great time cooking up some of these wonderful dishes.

I hope you have a great day and I wish you all the best.
If you could find the time to leave a review for my eBook, it would mean the world to me.

Made in the USA
Las Vegas, NV
14 September 2024

95278886R00090